The Best JESUS

written by Sheila Schuller Coleman

illustrated by John Ham

Second Edition, 1995
Library of Congress Catalog Card Number 88-63576
© 1989 by Sheila Schuller Coleman
Published by The Standard Publishing Company, Cincinnati, Ohio
A division of Standex International Corporation. Printed in U.S.A.

Nathanael, a shepherd boy, lived in Bethlehem a long, long time ago. He helped his father care for the sheep every day.

And Nathanael liked being a shepherd boy because at night he could listen to stories around the campfire.

The old shepherd storyteller told
exciting and wonderful stories. But
sometimes Nathanael got so excited, he
would interrupt the storyteller. When
he did, the old storyteller would remind
him that the story wasn't over until he
heard the word "Amen."

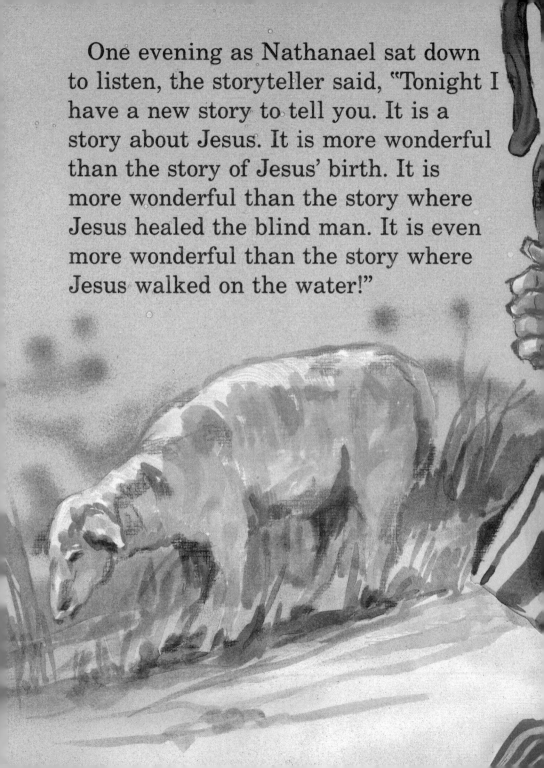

One evening as Nathanael sat down to listen, the storyteller said, "Tonight I have a new story to tell you. It is a story about Jesus. It is more wonderful than the story of Jesus' birth. It is more wonderful than the story where Jesus healed the blind man. It is even more wonderful than the story where Jesus walked on the water!"

Nathanael wondered what special story that could be. So he listened very closely as the old storyteller began. Nathanael wanted to hear every word he said.

"This story starts on a Sunday when the people were gathering in the great city of Jerusalem. They were coming from every town and city to celebrate the feast of Passover.

"Jesus and His twelve disciples also journeyed to Jerusalem for the Passover. And when Jesus entered the city, He was riding on a donkey.

"The people were so happy to see Jesus, they greeted Him like a king. They spread their coats and garments in the road for Him to ride over. They waved palm branches and shouted, 'Hosanna! Blessed is He who comes in the name of the Lord!'"

Nathanael liked the idea of Jesus being treated like a king. He was so excited, he said, "I like this story about Jesus!"

But the storyteller reminded him, "The story's not over yet, Nathanael. I haven't said, 'Amen.'"

Then the old shepherd continued the story, "The people had gathered in Jerusalem to eat the feast of Passover. It was a special time when all of God's people remembered His love and care for them.

"Jesus and His disciples wanted to celebrate Passover too. But the city was crowded. It would be difficult to find a room where they could be alone to eat their Passover supper. Jesus knew just the place — a large upper room in a house.

"And while they were eating, Jesus took some bread and some juice. He gave it to each of His disciples. As each man ate the bread and drank the juice, Jesus said, 'When you do this in years to come, remember me. And also remember how much I love you!'

"After the supper was over, Jesus and His friends went to a beautiful garden. The disciples heard Jesus pray, 'Father, I will do whatever it is You want me to do.'

"All of a sudden some soldiers burst into the garden. They arrested Jesus and took Him away."

Nathanael cried, "Oh! Why would anyone arrest Jesus? He didn't do anything bad!"

But the storyteller reminded him, "The story's not over yet, Nathanael. I haven't said, 'Amen.'"

The old shepherd continued the story, "The soldiers took Jesus to some men who wanted to kill Him. They gave Jesus an unfair trial and said He should die.

"Then the soldiers nailed Jesus to a cross. It was very painful. But Jesus understood that He needed to die for the sins of all people. He loved everyone. So He prayed to God, and then He died."

Nathanael cried, "No! No! Jesus didn't die! He lived!"

But the storyteller replied, "The story's not over yet, Nathanael. I haven't said, 'Amen.'"

Nathanael didn't like the story now. It was too sad. But he listened anyway as the storyteller continued, "Jesus' friends were very sad. They thought they would never see Jesus again. But two days later, three women went to the tomb where He had been buried.

"When they got there, they saw an amazing sight! The stone had been rolled away! The tomb was empty!

"Suddenly an angel appeared to the women and said, 'Jesus is not here! He is alive!'

"And the angel's words were true! A woman named Mary saw Jesus and talked to Him in the garden near the tomb.

"Two disciples walked with Him on the road to a town called Emmaus.

"Then Jesus appeared to all of His disciples as they were having dinner. He ate with them and talked with them.

"But soon Jesus knew it was time for Him to return to Heaven. His last words to His disciples were, 'Go into all the world and tell people everywhere that I love them.' And after this, Jesus was carried up to Heaven.

"The disciples did as Jesus asked. They went and preached throughout the world, telling everyone the greatest story of all — that Jesus lived, Jesus died, AND Jesus arose!"

And then the storyteller said, "Amen! Amen! and AMEN!"

When Nathanael heard the Amens, he cried, "And that's the end of the story!"

But the storyteller said, "Actually, Nathanael, that was just the beginning!"